MW01697782

# Social Studies Alive!®

## Me and My World

Third Edition

## Student Journal

**Welcome to your *Social Studies Alive!* Student Journal**

This journal is your place to read, reflect, and create. It works hand in hand with your online access.

In each lesson, you'll find:

- Preview Activity
- Vocabulary Activity
- Hands-On Activity
- Reading
- Show What You Know

In addition, look for the Activity Online callouts throughout the journal. These indicate that additional activity directions and interactions are online.

Every lesson also includes opportunities to dive deeper online, including:

- Lesson Games
- Vocabulary Cards
- Slideshows
- Videos and songs
- Primary Sources and more!

Sign in at **www.teachtci.com** to see all resources.

TCi™

CONTENTS

## Unit 1 History 1

Explore why you are special. Discover families and their traditions. Compare how life today has changed from the past. Conduct an inquiry to find out how your life might have been different long ago.



## Unit 2 Civics 47

Play the Sunshine Telephone game. Use puppets to learn how to make friends. Follow the "Let's Talk It Out!" method to solve problems. Go to good helper stations. Create a sash with holiday badges. Conduct an inquiry to help a new student at our school.

## Unit 3 Geography 123

Use map keys to find places on neighborhood maps. Make a telescope to show your city, state, country, and the world. Prepare for a cultural fair to show how people around the world live. Conduct an inquiry to discover your place in this world.



## Unit 4 Economics 175

Go on a shopping trip to pick out things you need and want. Use your environmental superhero powers to find ways to protect Earth. Conduct an inquiry to figure out how to meet your needs while also helping our world.

# A Whole New Way to Experience Social Studies

### Inquiry-Based Unit Structures

Each unit starts with an intriguing storyline and compelling question that piques students' interest and drives instruction throughout the lesson. They are encouraged to draw upon and apply previous knowledge and also use outside resources and Social Studies Stories to expand their answer.

### Student-Centered Activities

Each lesson utilizes at least one of TCI's unique, hands-on strategies to get students thinking, moving, and asking big questions. Students are inspired to learn more and engage in fun activities, which they can access both online and in the Journal.

### Engage All Learners

Meaningful standards-aligned content with opportunities for making personal connections and exploring diverse perspectives.

### Online Resources

Ready-to-teach presentations, activities, complete student resources, customizable assessments and more at your fingertips!

## Unit 1

# History

Explore why you are special. Discover families and their traditions. Compare how life today has changed from the past. Conduct an inquiry to find out how your life might have been different long ago.

# Unit Inquiry Project

## 1 Gathering Visual Evidence

| | |
|---|---|
| List five things you see in this photograph. | |
| What looks the same as today? | |
| What looks different from today? | |

 

## 2 Developing the Compelling Question

### Unit Storyline

This photo shows a family on a farm. It was taken over 100 years ago! The farm was in Nebraska. Some things today are the same as long ago. Some things today are different from long ago.

### Unit Compelling Question

*What would my life have been like long ago?*

List three questions you have about the Unit Storyline and Compelling Question.

1.

2.

3.

## 3 Collecting Evidence

After you complete each lesson, return to this table and answer the questions. Record key information that will help you complete the Unit Inquiry Project.

| Lesson | Supporting Questions | What I Learned |
|---|---|---|
| **1 Who Am I?** | Look at the photo of the farm again. Do you think the people cared for each other? Do you think they had feelings? How else might they be similar to you today? | |
| **2 What Is a Family?** | What traditions might the family on the farm have had?<br><br>Ask an adult at home: What traditions did your family have long ago? | |
| **3 How Is Our Life Different from Long Ago?** | How did the family on the farm get water? How did they travel?<br><br>Ask an adult at home: How might you have traveled long ago? How else might your life have been different or the same? | |

## 4 Building Additional Content Knowledge

Gather and evaluate additional sources to answer the Unit Compelling Question: *What would my life have been like long ago?*

You may conduct research or use these readings from *Social Studies Alive! Me and My World* Social Studies Stories:

- The Story of Our Flag
- Our Country's Birthday
- The First Thanksgiving
- Birthdays Then and Now

| | |
|---|---|
| Source Title(s) | |
| Additional Evidence | |

## 5 Constructing an Argument

Write a sentence answering the Unit Compelling Question: *What would my life have been like long ago?* This is called a claim.

Then give at least two pieces of evidence to support your claim. Your evidence can come from the activities you did in class, the readings you completed in your Student Journal or Social Studies Stories, or additional research that you conducted.

**Claim:**

**Evidence:**

## 6 Taking Informed Action

Decide how you want to share what you learned. You could make a poster, a presentation, or a video. You might share your presentation with your classmates or with adults in the community.

# Lesson 1

# Who Am I?

How am I special?

No one looks like me.

No one talks like me.

**Vocabulary**

**feelings**

**special**

## Preview Activity

Activity Online

Finish the words to the "Everyone Is Special" song.

Some kids like to

jump !

Some kids like to

dance !

Some kids like to

run !

## Vocabulary Activity

Activity Online

Trace the word under each picture.

feelings

special

## Hands-On Activity

Use facial expressions to guess how someone might be feeling in different situations.

### Directions: Exploring Feelings

1. **Read Sections 1 and 2.** Learn about being special and caring.
2. **Find out why good citizens consider people's feelings.** Analyze photos of students talking to each other.
3. **Think of more feelings you can name.** Try to show them with your face.
4. **Practice showing feelings together.** Your teacher will say a feeling and then count to three. On the count of three, show what the feeling looks like.
5. **Meet Lorena and then play a game.** For each image, guess how Lorena is feeling. Then find out!
6. **Read Sections 3 and 4 and complete your Activity Notes.** Learn about feelings and doing things.

## 1. Being Special

I am **special**.

No one looks the way I look.

No one likes all the things I like.

There is only one me.

## 2. Caring

I care about my family.

To show I care, I give them hugs.

I care about my friends, too.

We help each other out.

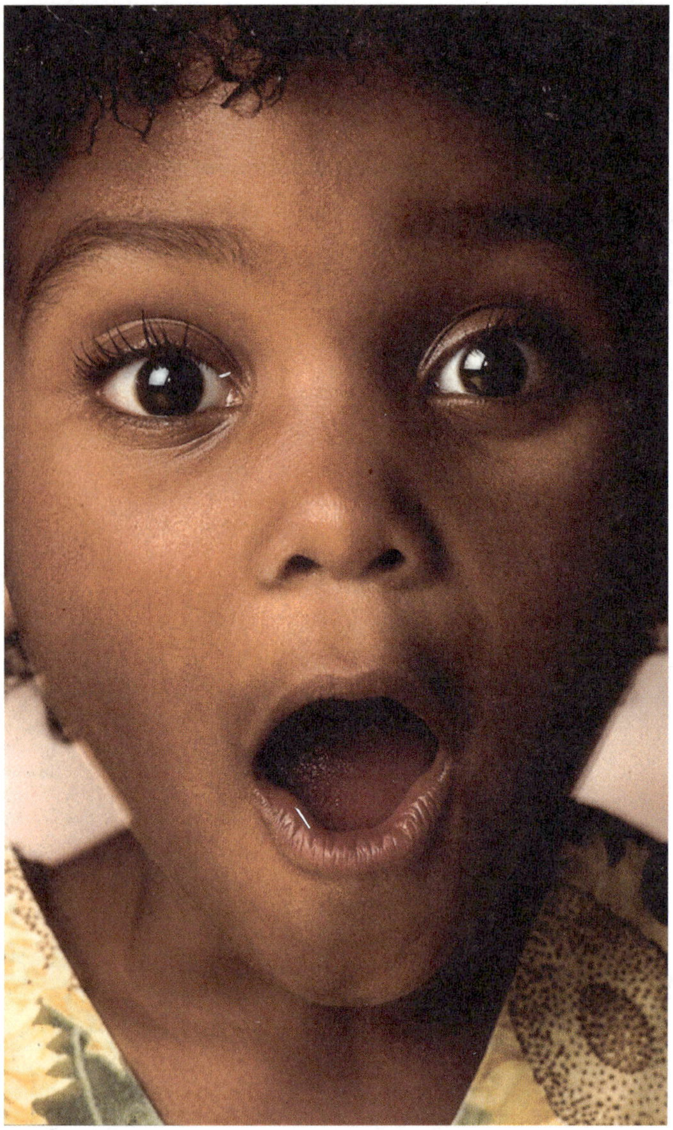 

## 3. Feelings

I have many **feelings**.

I can feel happy. I smile.

I can feel angry or sad, too.

Sometimes I am surprised.

## 4. Doing Many Things

I can do many things.

At school, I draw and sing.

I play sports with friends.

At home, I talk to my family.

## Hands-On Activity Notes

Activity Online

Draw how you feel when each of these things happens to you.

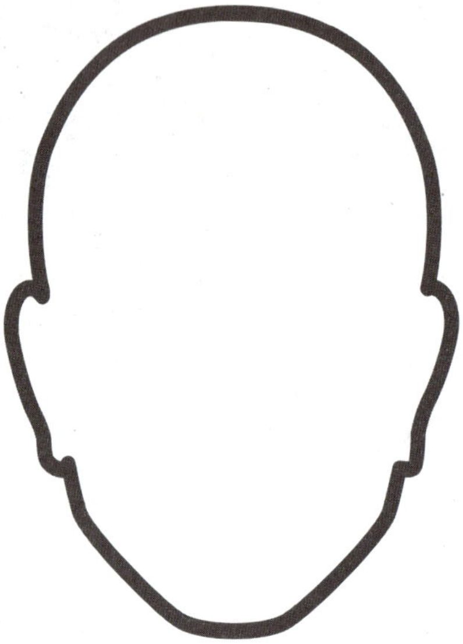

You broke something.

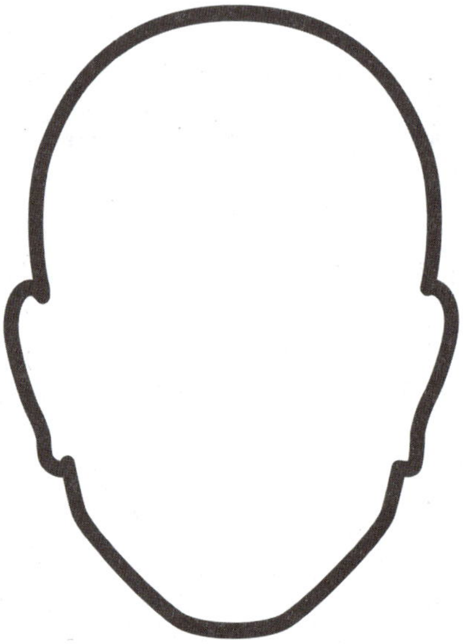

You have a birthday party!

Feelings change during the day.

Draw things that you do on the timeline.

Draw how you feel when you do each one.

**7** **A.M.** | **12** **P.M.** | **4** **P.M.**

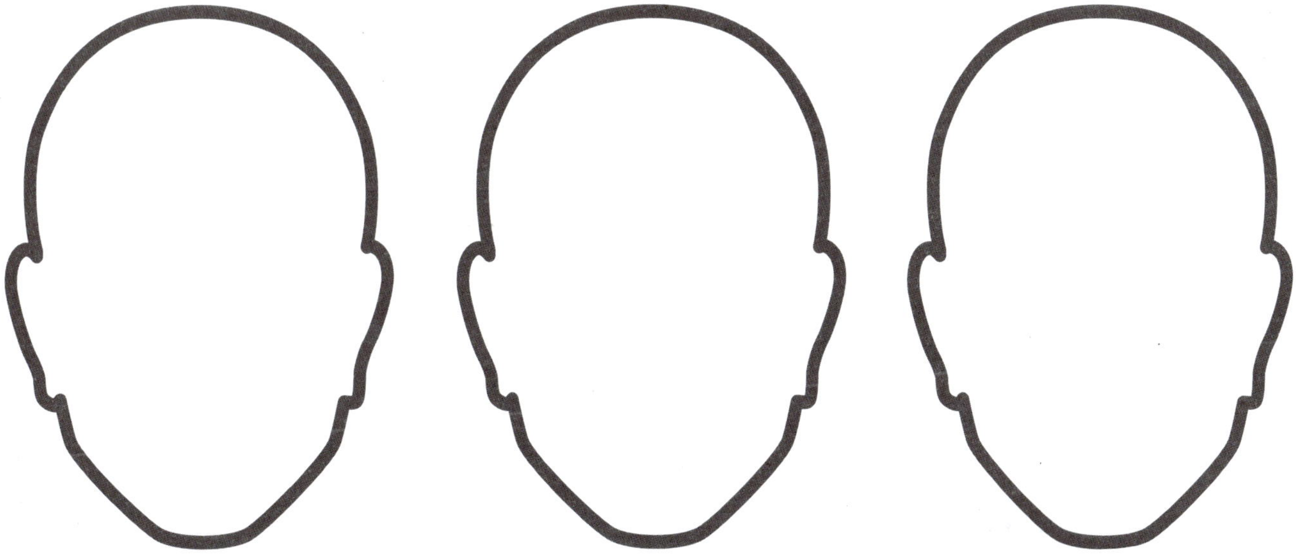

## Summary

I am special.

I can do many things.

## Show What You Know

Draw your face. Draw two things that make you special.

1

2

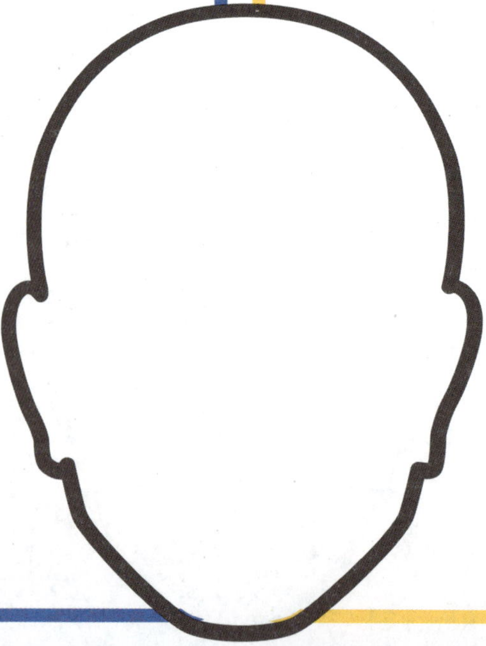

# Lesson 2

# What Is a Family?

I live with my family.

We care for each other.

We do things together.

**Vocabulary**

**family**

**tradition**

## Preview Activity

Activity Online

Draw your family.

## Vocabulary Activity

Activity Online

Trace the word under each picture.

family

tradition

## Hands-On Activity

Match cultural objects to family traditions during six holidays: Independence Day, Chinese New Year, Thanksgiving, Divali, Christmas, and Day of the Dead.

### Directions: Discovering Traditions

1. **Read Sections 1–4.** Learn about families.
2. **You and your partner will be given an object.** It is used by one of the families during their holiday celebration.
3. **Then, as a class, we will visit six families. Does your object match with the family's tradition?**
4. **If you think you have a match, jump up to the screen and explain why.** Give evidence.
5. **Read Sections 5–7.** Learn about other traditions!

## 1. My Family

I am part of a **family**.

I live with people in my family.

We spend time together.

We all love each other.

## 2. Caring

Families take care of each other.

Adults take care of children.

Sometimes brothers and sisters

help take care of each other, too.

## 3. Doing Things Together

Families do things together.

They go for bike rides.

Sometimes they play board games.

What else do families do together?

## 4. Traditions

Families have **traditions**.

A tradition is something that a

family has done for many years.

Many holidays have traditions.

## 5. A Birthday Tradition

Families celebrate birthdays.

Some fill a piñata with treats.

Someone breaks it open.

The treats fall to the ground.

## 6. A Fall Tradition

Some families eat moon cakes.

The cakes are pastries filled with lotus.

Families eat them for a fall festival.

They celebrate food and family.

## 7. Valentine's Day Traditions

Schools have traditions, too.

We celebrate Valentine's Day.

I give a card to each classmate.

This shows I care about others.

## Hands-On Activity Notes

Activity Online

Draw a picture of one of your family's holiday traditions. Write the name of the holiday.

## Summary

A family cares about one another.

My family is special.

### Show What You Know

Draw a picture of a new family tradition you could start. Be sure to color the frame!

# Lesson 3

## How Is Our Life Different from Long Ago?

Would you have liked to live long ago? Things were different. Primary sources show us how.

**Vocabulary**

**travel**

**well**

## Preview Activity

Activity Online

# What do you want to know about long ago?

Write a question.

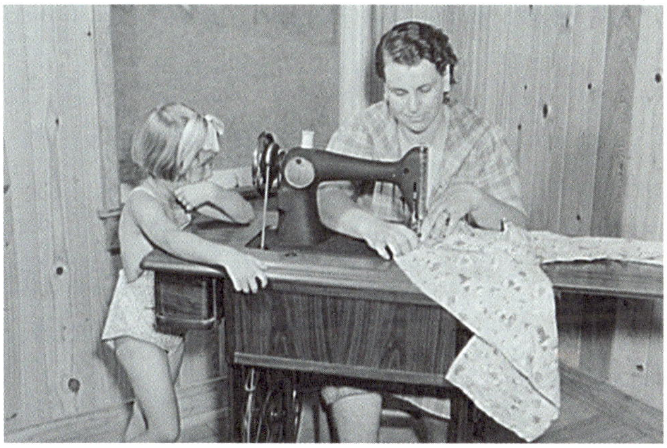

## Vocabulary Activity

Activity Online

Trace the word under each picture.

travel

well

## Hands-On Activity

Predict what will happen in videos about getting water long ago and today. Visit six stations to categorize transportation as being from the past or today.

### Directions: Getting Water

1. **For each video, follow the steps on the slide.** Predict what will happen. Then watch the ending to see how people got water long ago and today.
2. **Read Sections 1 and 2.** Learn that the way people get water and clothes has changed. Complete your activity notes.

### Directions: Comparing How We Travel

1. **Look at the card your teacher has given you.** It might be an airplane, boat, train, bus, car, or truck!
2. **When your type of transportation is on the slide, show your card to the class.** Then put all of the cards for that type of transportation together.
3. **At the six stations around the room, sort the pictures.** Make two groups about how we go places: Long Ago and Today.
4. **Read Sections 3–4 and complete your Activity Notes.** Learn how transportation has changed over time.

## 1. We Get Water

People always need water to drink and wash.

Long ago, people took water from rivers and streams.

Then people built **wells**. They pulled water up in buckets. Now people go to a sink. They get water easily.

## Hands-On Activity Notes

Activity Online

Look at the timeline.

Write **Long Ago** in the correct place.

Write **Today** in the correct place.

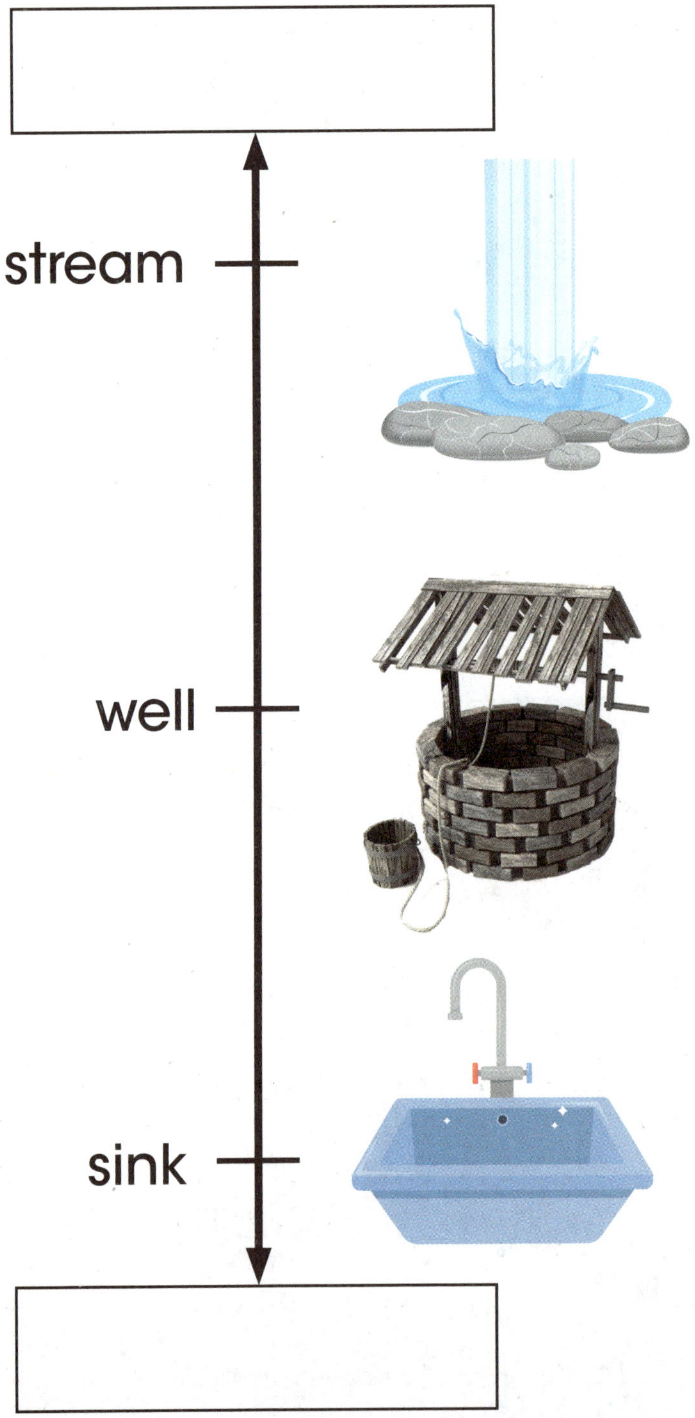

## 2. We Get Clothes

Long ago, people made all their clothes.

Today, we can also buy clothes in stores.

## 3. We Go Places

The ways we **travel** have changed.

Long ago, people used horses to go places.

Then people made cars.

But cars from long ago look

different from cars today.

So do planes and trains.

## Hands-On Activity Notes

Activity Online

Look at each picture. Circle if it shows how to go places long ago or today.

Long Ago Today

Long Ago Today

Long Ago Today

Long Ago Today

Long Ago Today

Long Ago Today

## 4. We Work

At work, we use computers and smartphones to write each other. Long ago, people used pen and paper. Some used typewriters.

## Summary

Some things long ago were the same as today.

Some things were different.

### Show What You Know

Look at each drawing. Circle if it is from long ago or from today.

Long Ago Today

Long Ago Today

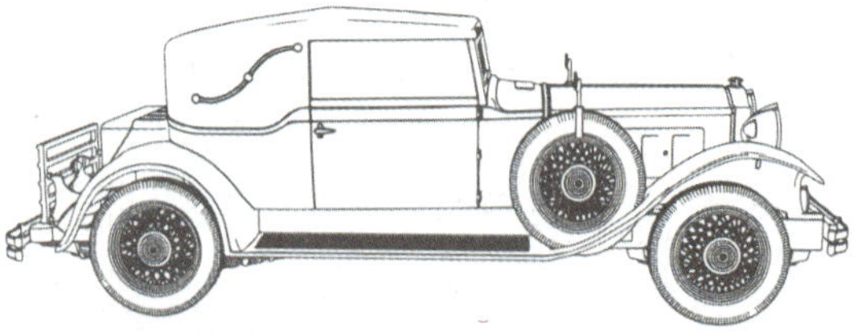

Long Ago Today

Long Ago Today

Unit 2

# Civics

Play the Sunshine Telephone game. Use puppets to learn how to make friends. Follow the "Let's Talk It Out!" method to solve problems. Go to good helper stations. Create a sash with holiday badges. Conduct an inquiry to help a new student at our school.

# Unit Inquiry Project

## 1 Gathering Visual Evidence

| | |
|---|---|
| List five things you see in this image. | |
| What do you think is happening? | |
| How do you think this new student feels? Why? | |

## 2 Developing the Compelling Question

**Unit Storyline**

A new student has just arrived at our school. She is excited but a little bit scared. She wonders, "Where do I put my things in the morning? When do we go to recess? How do I make friends?"

**Unit Compelling Question**

*How can I help a new student at our school?*

List three questions you have about the Unit Storyline and Compelling Question.

1.

2.

3.

## 3 Collecting Evidence

After you complete each lesson, return to this table and answer the questions. Record key information that will help you complete the Unit Inquiry Project.

| Lesson | Supporting Questions | What I Learned |
|---|---|---|
| **4 How Do I Get Along with Others?** | How can we help a new student feel welcome? | |
| **5 How Do I Make Friends?** | How can we help a new student make friends? | |
| **6 How Do I Solve Problems with Others?** | How can we help a new student work well with others? | |
| **7 How Can I Be a Good Helper at School?** | How can we model being a good helper for a new student? | |
| **8 How Do Americans Celebrate?** | What are some ways we celebrate America? | |

## 4 Building Additional Content Knowledge

Gather and evaluate additional sources to answer the Unit Compelling Question: *How can I help a new student at our school?*

You may conduct research or use these readings from *Social Studies Alive! Me and My World* Social Studies Stories:

- Rules Help Us
- Who Can Help?
- Dr. King Fights for Rights

| | |
|---|---|
| Source Title(s) | |
| Additional Evidence | |

## 5 Constructing an Argument

Write a sentence answering the Unit Compelling Question: *How can I help a new student at our school?* This is called a claim.

Then give at least two pieces of evidence to support your claim. Your evidence can come from the activities you did in class, the readings you completed in your Student Journal or Social Studies Stories, or additional research that you conducted.

**Claim:**

**Evidence:**

## 6 Taking Informed Action

Decide how you want to share what you learned. You could make a poster, a presentation, or a video. You might share your presentation with your classmates or with adults in the community.

# Lesson 4

# How Do I Get Along with Others?

I try to get along.

I am a good listener.

I take turns.

**Vocabulary**

**get along**

## Preview Activity

Activity Online

For each situation:

- Draw an open mouth on the monster friend who should be talking.
- Draw a closed mouth on the monster friend who should be listening.

Blue and Orange are in class, and their teacher is giving directions.

Orange needs to practice saying a poem.

Orange said something that hurt Blue's feelings.

Orange learned a funny joke and wants to tell it.

## Vocabulary Activity

Activity Online

Complete the image. Trace the letters in ***get along*** on the banner.

## Hands-On Activity

Play the Sunshine Telephone game to compete against your classmates and practice talking, listening, and taking turns.

### Directions: Playing the Sunshine Telephone Game

1. **Follow the teacher's instructions to get into place.** Your teacher will be the sun, and your group will be lined up like rays of sunlight.
2. **Listen carefully!** If you are the first team member of your group, your teacher will whisper a secret message into your ear.
3. **Pass the message along.** When your teacher says "Go," whisper the message into the ear of the person behind you and then sit down. Each team member should repeat this until all team members have heard the message.
4. **Reveal the secret message!** If you are the final team member in your sunshine ray, share the message you heard with the class.
5. **Play again!** Take turns listening to the secret message first.
6. **Then read Sections 1–4 and complete your Activity Notes.**

## 1. Talking

I talk when it is my turn.

I do not talk while others talk.

In class, I raise my hand.

Then I can answer questions.

## 2. Listening

I listen while others talk.

How am I a good listener?

I face the person talking to me.

I only talk when they are done.

## 3. Taking Turns

I take turns with others.

Sometimes, I wait in line.

I get to go, and then you go.

This helps us **get along**.

## Hands-On Activity Notes

Activity Online

Draw a picture of a good listener.

When someone talks to me,
I listen.

## 4. Making Choices

I make good choices.

I help a friend who is hurt.

If I make a mess, I clean it up.

I share my toys.

I help with the dishes.

Sometimes, I walk the dog.

I sit with the new student at lunch.

What other choices do I make?

## Summary

I talk, listen, and take turns.

I make good choices.

### Show What You Know

What is one good choice you make?

Draw a picture.

# Lesson 5

## How Do I Make Friends?

How do I make friends?

I talk to others.

I play with them, too.

**Vocabulary**

**introduce**

## Preview Activity

Activity Online

Draw a happy face to show someone who has found a friend. Draw a sad face to show someone who needs a friend.

## Vocabulary Activity

Activity Online

Circle the images that show good ways to **introduce** yourself to others.

## Hands-On Activity

Activity Online

Join a group of three and play with three puppets—Batty, Puffin, and Red Panda—to learn how to make friends.

### Directions: Puppets Introduce Themselves and Play

1. **Read Sections 1–2 and complete your Activity Notes.**
2. **Sit with your team of three and make your puppet.** Attach your character to the end of a pencil or craft stick with tape.
3. **Practice holding your puppet.** Hold the puppet out in front of you so your group can see it.
4. **Practice making your puppet's voice special.** What do you think your character would sound like if they could talk?
5. **Prepare to act out a scene.** Listen carefully to the instructions. Then use your puppets to act it out!

### Directions: Puppets Share and Are Kind

1. **Get your puppet out again, and sit with your team.**
2. **Practice being your puppet's character.**
3. **Prepare to act.** Listen carefully to the instructions. Use your puppets to act out each scene.
4. **Then read Sections 3–4 and complete your Activity Notes.**

## 1. Introducing Myself

I **introduce** myself to others.

First, I tell them my name.

Then, they tell me theirs.

I am polite and smile.

## 2. Asking Friends to Play

I ask a friend to play

blocks with me.

She may say "yes."

She may kindly say "no."

## Hands-On Activity Notes

Activity Online

Introduce yourself to three people.

Who did you introduce yourself to?

Write their names below.

1. ______________________________

2. ______________________________

3. ______________________________

## 3. Sharing

I share with others at school.

We share toys, books,

tape, and colored markers.

What else can we share?

## 4. Being Kind

I am kind to others.

I treat everyone the same.

At school, I help my classmates.

This makes me a good friend.

## Hands-On Activity Notes

Activity Online

Draw a picture showing you being kind to or sharing with a friend.

## Summary

I introduce myself.

I share. I am kind.

### Show What You Know

Introduce yourself by completing the sentence.

Then draw a picture of yourself.

Hello, I am ______________________________.

# Lesson 6

# How Do I Solve Problems with Others?

We have a problem.

How can we fix it?

We solve it together.

## Vocabulary

**calm down**

**problem**

**solve**

**vote**

## Preview Activity

Activity Online

Circle the pictures that show someone having a problem.

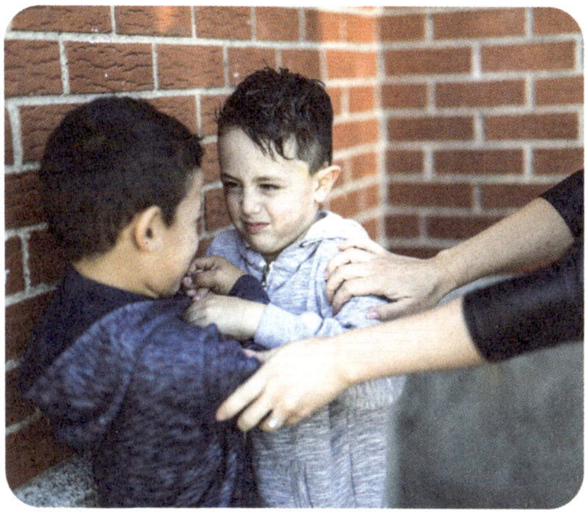

## Vocabulary Activity

Activity Online

What are four ways you can solve problems with others? Complete the sentences.

Stop and calm down.

Say what the problem is.

Solve it by thinking of solutions.

Vote on which solution is best.

## Hands-On Activity

Activity Online

Listen to a story about the lion family and discuss four steps the family might take to solve a problem. Use the four-step "Let's Talk It Out!" method to help solve problems with others.

### Directions: Creating a Way to Solve Problems with Others

1. **Listen to the story about the lion family.**
2. **Act out how the family members feel.** Show what Baby, Mama, and Papa are feeling.
3. **Use the "Let's Talk It Out!" card to come up with solutions.**
4. **Then read Sections 1–4 and complete your Activity Notes.**

### Directions: Practicing Solving Problems with Others

1. **With your partner, watch each of the videos.** Discuss what you see happening in each video.
2. **Discuss how the children could solve their problems.** Use the "Let's Talk It Out!" steps to help.
3. **Prepare a quick skit.** Your skit should show what the problem is and what the students could do to solve their problems.
4. **Act out your skit if called upon.** Be sure to include the steps you took to solve the problem.
5. **Then read Sections 5–6 and complete your Activity Notes.**

## 1. Calming Down

My friend and I have a **problem**.

We both want the same marker.

I feel upset. What can we do?

First, I stop and **calm down**.

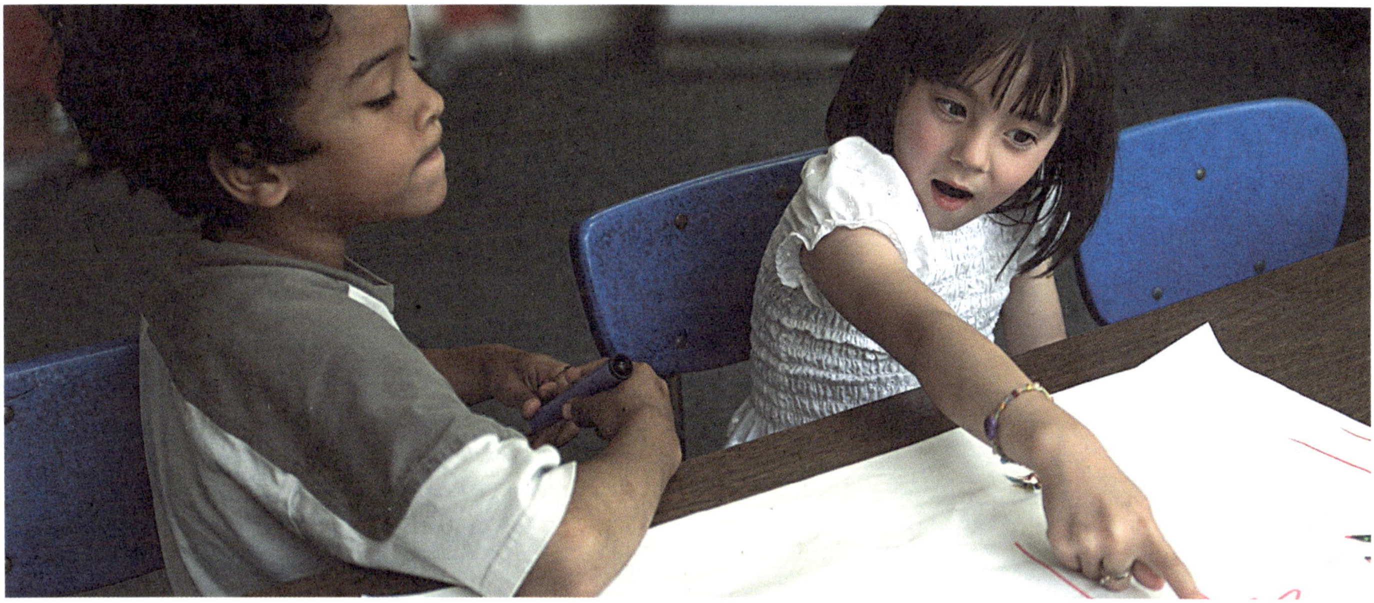

## 2. Talking and Listening

Next, we listen and talk.

I say why my feelings are hurt.

Then, my friend does the same.

We listen to each other.

## 3. Solving Problems

Now, we think of ways

to **solve** the problem.

I share my ideas.

Then, you share yours.

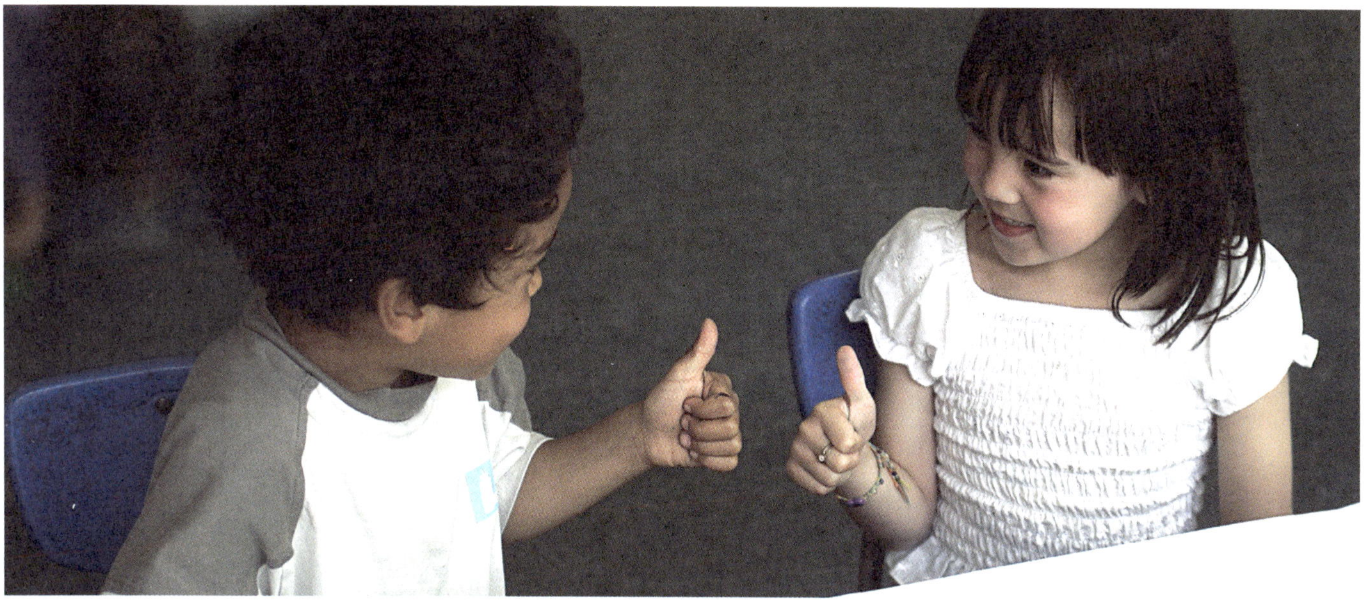

## 4. Trying a Plan

We agree on a plan.

Then, we try it.

If our plan does not work,

we can try another plan.

## Hands-On Activity Notes

Activity Online

Trace the number and the first word for each step.

1 Stop and Calm Down

2 Listen and Talk

3 Think of Solutions

4 Vote on a Plan and Try It

## 5. Solving Problems in Class

Our class solves problems, too.

Some of us want to make robots.

Some of us want to put on a play.

What can we do?

## 6. Voting

We can **vote** on what to do.

I raise my hand for my choice.

The most votes wins.

We will put on a play!

## Hands-On Activity Notes

Activity Online

Think of a time you and your friends, family, or classmates solved a problem.

Draw a picture of the problem. Then draw a picture of the solution.

PROBLEM

SOLUTION

## Summary

I stop and calm down.

I think of ways to solve the problem.

## Show What You Know

Draw an image for each of the steps.

① Stop and Calm Down

② Listen and Talk

③ Think of Solutions

④ Vote on a Plan and Try It

**Lesson 7**

# How Can I Be a Good Helper at School?

We can help at school.

Then it is a better place.

How can I help?

**Vocabulary**

**directions**

## Preview Activity

Activity Online

Mr. Patel is giving examples of times when his students were good helpers.

Draw a smile on his face when he gives examples of good helpers.

## Vocabulary Activity

Activity Online

Trace the vocabulary word under each picture.

She is following directions.

They are not following directions.

## Hands-On Activity

Visit eight stations that challenge you to take care of things, clean up, follow directions, or do your work.

### Directions: You Can Make School a Better Place

1. **Read Sections 1–4.** Learn how you can be a good helper at school.
2. **With your partner, start by visiting one of the stations around the room.** At the station:
   - Look at the Activity Card and discuss what it shows.
   - Put the missing pieces of the Activity Card where they belong.
   - Check your work by finding the picture of the Activity Card in your Student Journal. Then complete your Activity Notes by filling in the blanks.
   - Show your work to your teacher and go to the next station.
3. **Visit as many stations as you can.** Complete the steps for each station you visit.
4. **Then check your work as a class and complete your Activity Notes.**

## 1. Taking Care of Things

I help take care of things.

I treat objects with care

so they will last longer.

I feed the class pet.

## Hands-On Activity Notes

Activity Online

### Station A: Taking Care of the Class Pets

I help take care of the class ______.

### Station B: Taking Care of the Bookshelves

I put __________ away on the correct bookshelves.

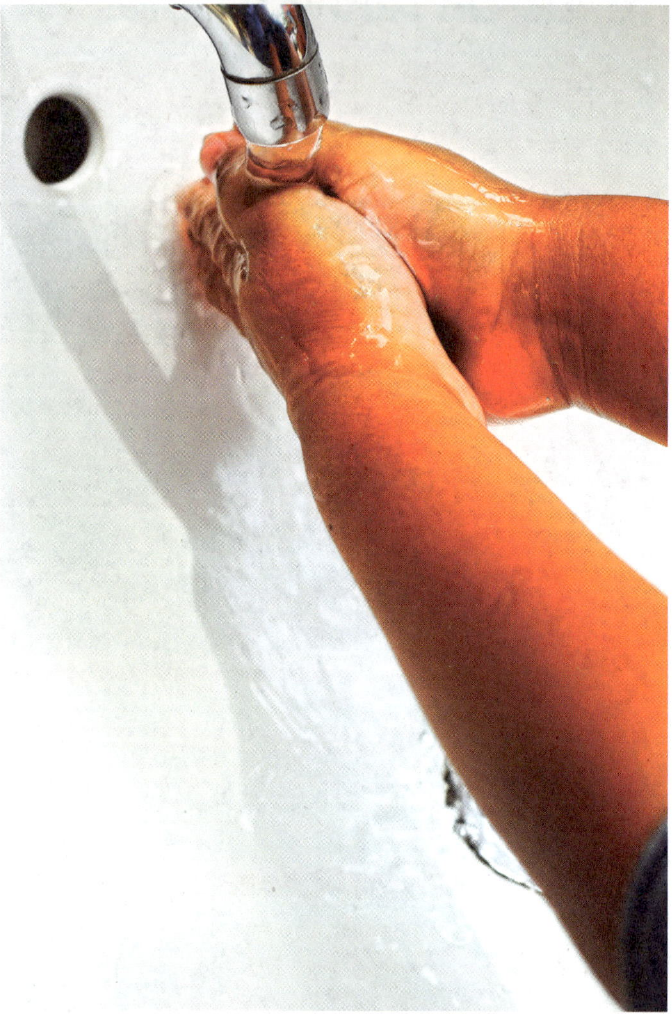

## 2. Cleaning Up

I help keep my school clean.

After I use something,

I put it away. I wash up.

I throw away my trash.

# Hands-On Activity Notes

Activity Online

## Station C: Cleaning Up After an Art Project

I clean up after an _____ project.

## Station D: Cleaning Up After Lunch

I clean up after __________.

## 3. Following Directions

I listen to my teacher and

follow **directions**.

Then I know what to do.

I obey the school rules.

## Hands-On Activity Notes

Activity Online

### Station E: Following Directions When You Arrive at School

I follow ________________ when I arrive at school.

### Station F: Obeying the School Rules

I obey the school ________.

## 4. Doing My Work

I do my work so I can learn.

I ask questions.

I finish my work on time.

I work well with others.

## Hands-On Activity Notes

Activity Online

### Station G: Learning My Letters So I Can Read

I learn my __________ so I can read.

### Station H: Learning My Numbers So I Can Count

I learn my ____________ so I can count.

## Summary

I take care of things.

I do my work.

### Show What You Know

Put away items around the classroom.

Complete the picture by drawing classroom items.

# Lesson 8

# How Do Americans Celebrate?

We live in the United
States of America.
We are proud Americans.

**Vocabulary**
**federal holiday**
**patriotic**

 

**Preview Activity**

Activity Online

# Can you match the holiday images?

## Vocabulary Activity

Activity Online

Trace the word under each picture.

Christmas is a federal holiday.

They are patriotic.

## Hands-On Activity

Activity Online

View videos about five federal holidays in the United States and pick a badge to represent each on your sash. Then see photographs of statues representing past Americans whom we celebrate with federal holidays and pick a badge for each. Add those to your sash.

### Directions: Five Special American Holidays

1. **Cut out your badges with your partner.** Do you recognize any pictures on the badges?
2. **Watch a video about a special American holiday.** After the video, discuss what you saw.
3. **Pick a badge to represent the federal holiday shown in the video.** You will have five badges to pick from. Can you match the correct video with the correct badge?
4. **Glue the badge to your sash.** Repeat Steps 2–4 until you have five new badges on your sash.
5. **Then read Section 1.**

### Directions: Six Holidays to Help Us Remember

1. **Cut out your badges with your partner.** Do you recognize any pictures on the badges?
2. **Look at the photograph while you listen to the story behind it.** Then discuss what you learned.
3. **Pick a badge to represent the federal holiday you heard about.** You will have six badges to pick from. Can you pick the correct badge?
4. **Glue the badge to your sash.** Repeat Steps 2–4 until you have six new badges on your sash.
5. **Then read Sections 2–4.**

## 1. We Celebrate Federal Holidays

The Fourth of July is the day the United States was born. We wave flags in parades.

We celebrate Thanksgiving. We share a special meal with friends and family. These are **federal holidays** we celebrate.

## 2. We Celebrate Great Leaders

We celebrate the birthdays of important leaders. Happy birthday, presidents Washington and Lincoln! Lincoln's nickname was "Honest Abe." Happy birthday, Dr. King!

There are special days to celebrate others. There is a day for César Chávez. What leaders are important to your community? How could you learn more about them?

## 3. We Tell Stories

We tell stories about people who lived long ago. Pocahontas was the daughter of a powerful Native American leader. She helped people in an early English colony.

Harriett Tubman was born an enslaved African American. She escaped and helped other enslaved people. Daniel Boone was a pioneer. He made new mountain trails. He helped settlers move to Kentucky.

## 4. We Sing Songs

Do you know the song

"This Land Is Your Land?"

Are you a proud American?

If you are proud of your country,

you are **patriotic**.

## Summary

The United States has 11 federal holidays.

We celebrate special days in the year.

### Show What You Know

Draw a symbol for each of these three holidays.

Look at the calendar. Order the holidays. Write the words *first, next,* and *last* to show the order.

| Federal Holiday | Order |
|---|---|
| Independence Day | |
| Martin Luther King Jr. Day | |
| Thanksgiving Day | |

## Activity Cutouts

Activity Online

Cut out these badges to make your federal holiday sash.

Cut out these badges.

Tear out this page when you are ready to make your sash.

## Activity Cutouts

Activity Online

# Cut out these badges for your holiday sash.

Cut out these badges.

Tear out this page when you are ready to make your sash.

Unit 3

# Geography

Use map keys to find places on neighborhood maps. Make a telescope to show your city, state, country, and the world. Prepare for a cultural fair to show how people around the world live. Conduct an inquiry to discover your place in this world.

# Unit Inquiry Project

## 1 Gathering Visual Evidence

| | |
|---|---|
| List five things you see in this video. | |
| What happens during the video? Where do you start? Where do you end up? | |
| What are some ways to describe the different places you see in the video? | |

## 2 Developing the Compelling Question

### Unit Storyline

The video begins in a neighborhood in New York City. As we get farther away from the ground, the buildings seem to be getting smaller and smaller. We can't see them any longer. All we can see is land and water. As we move farther away into space, we can see the whole world! What would it look like if we started at your school and then got farther away into space?

### Unit Compelling Question

*Where is my place in the world?*

List three questions you have about the Unit Storyline and Compelling Question.

1.

2.

3.

## 3 Collecting Evidence

After you complete each lesson, return to this table and answer the questions. Record key information that will help you complete the Unit Inquiry Project.

| Lesson | Supporting Questions | What I Learned |
|---|---|---|
| **9 What Is in My Neighborhood?** | What is a map? What kinds of things in your neighborhood can you see on a map? Who are your neighbors? | |
| **10 Where Am I in the World?** | What city do you live in? What state do you live in? What country do you live in? | |
| **11 How Do People Live Around the World?** | What similarities do you have with people all over the world?<br><br>Now think about your local area. What languages are spoken? How do children eat and play? What music do you listen to? | |

## 4 Building Additional Content Knowledge

Gather and evaluate additional sources to answer the Unit Compelling Question: *Where is my place in the world?*

You may conduct research or use these readings from *Social Studies Alive! Me and My World* Social Studies Stories:

- Who Works at My School?
- Symbols of Our Country

| | |
|---|---|
| Source Title(s) | |
| Additional Evidence | |

## 5 Constructing an Argument

Write a sentence answering the Unit Compelling Question: *Where is my place in the world?* This is called a claim.

Then give at least two pieces of evidence to support your claim. Your evidence can come from the activities you did in class, the readings you completed in your Student Journal or Social Studies Stories, or additional research that you conducted.

**Claim:**

**Evidence:**

## 6 Taking Informed Action

Decide how you want to share what you learned. You could make a poster, a presentation, or a video. You might share your presentation with your classmates or with adults in the community.

Lesson 9

# What Is in My Neighborhood?

People live and work

in my neighborhood.

I live here, too.

**Vocabulary**

**map**

**neighbor**

**neighborhood**

## Preview Activity

Activity Online

Can you match each object with its symbol?

**Pool**

**Palm tree**

**Hotel**

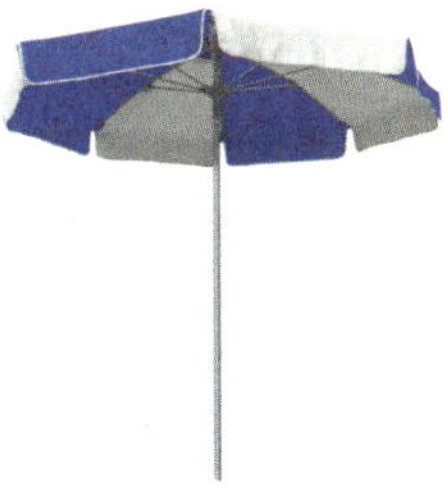

**Umbrella**

## Vocabulary Activity

Activity Online

Read the story. Trace the word to finish each sentence.

### A Trip to a New Place

I live in a big city. I am going to visit my friend. He lives in a different neighborhood. I look at the subway map. The map helps me find my way. When I get there, I meet my friend's neighbors.

## Hands-On Activity

Activity Online

Use a map key to find eight places in a neighborhood. Then fill in a map key to show eight different places on a neighborhood map.

### Directions: Finding Places

1. **With your partner, place the chip your teacher gave you on the map in your Activity Notes.**
2. **Listen to each task. Move your chip to the correct location on the map.** Your teacher will click a button online and read the task. Move your chip around the neighborhood map to answer the task.
3. **You will complete eight tasks in total.** Can you answer them all correctly?
4. **Then read Sections 1–2.**

### Directions: Making a Map Key

1. **With your partner, collect eight different colored crayons, markers, or pencils.**
2. **When your teacher asks, hold a color up in the air.**
3. **In your Activity Notes, use that same color to color the pool on the map and the box next to the word *Pool.*** You are making a map key!
4. **Continue filling in your map and map key using your seven other colors.**
5. **Then read Sections 3–4.**

## Hands-On Activity Notes

Activity Online

Move your chip to complete each task.

### Map Key

- Library
- Kenisha's home
- Pool
- Umbrella
- Fountain
- Intersection
- Palm tree

## 1. Buildings Where I Live

My **neighborhood** has buildings.

There are many homes.

I live in an apartment.

My friend lives in a house.

There are stores and schools, too.

There is a sign over the bank door.

People sit in front of the cafe.

Tables are under the umbrellas.

## 2. Outdoors Where I Live

A neighborhood has outdoor areas.

My dad and I sit near the pond.

I slide behind friends at the park.

My friends run along the paths.

We go sledding in winter.

We have picnics in spring.

We garden in summer.

We jump in leaf piles in fall.

## Hands-On Activity Notes

Activity Online

Follow along with your class. Color in the map and key to complete the map.

**Map Key**

| | | | |
|---|---|---|---|
| A | Pool | E | Hospital |
| B | Library | F | Apartments |
| C | Fire department | G | Post office |
| D | Grocery store | H | Soccer field |

**A Neighborhood Map**

## 3. Neighborhood Maps

**Map Key**

- Land
- Water
- Road

A **map** shows what a place looks like from above.

What does the map key show?

Land is green. Water is blue.

## My Neighborhood Map

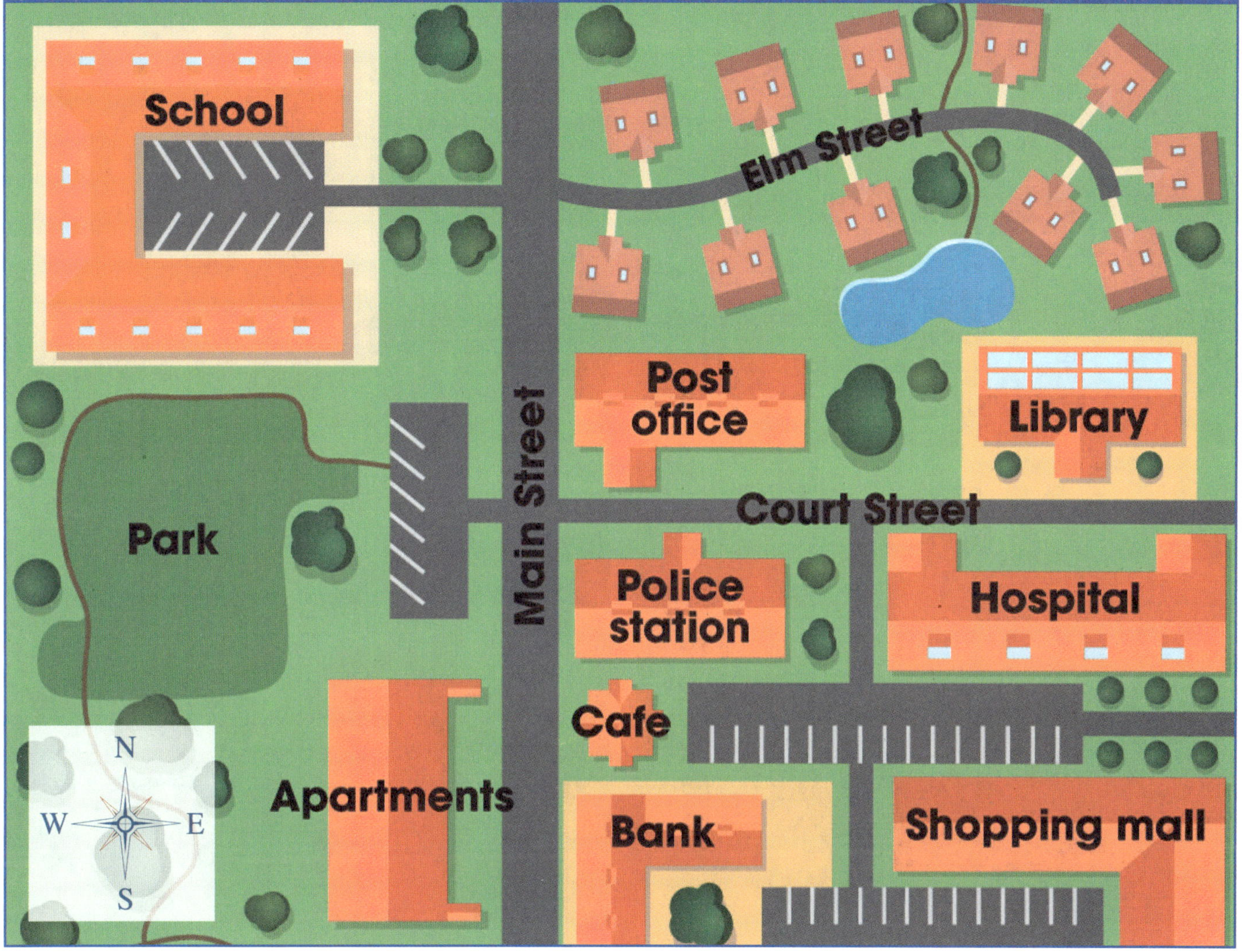


I can use a map to find things.

The school is near the park.

The pond is far from the apartments.

A compass rose shows directions.

The cafe is north of the bank.

**Map Key**

- Land
- Water
- Road

## 4. My Neighbors

My neighborhood has people.

The people who live and work nearby

are my **neighbors**.

My neighbors are all different.

Some neighbors are old and tall.

Some are young and small.

I am part of my neighborhood!

Who are your neighbors?

## Summary

I live in a neighborhood.

I can draw a map of places there.

### Show What You Know

Add four places to this map. Complete the map key to identify the four places.

**Map Key**

| | |
|---|---|
| ☐ ________________ | ☐ ________________ |
| ☐ ________________ | ☐ ________________ |

# Lesson 10

# Where Am I in the World?

The world is a big place.

Where do I live?

I can find it on a globe.

**Vocabulary**

**city**

**country**

**state**

**world**

 

**Preview Activity**

Activity Online

Write the missing words from the song.

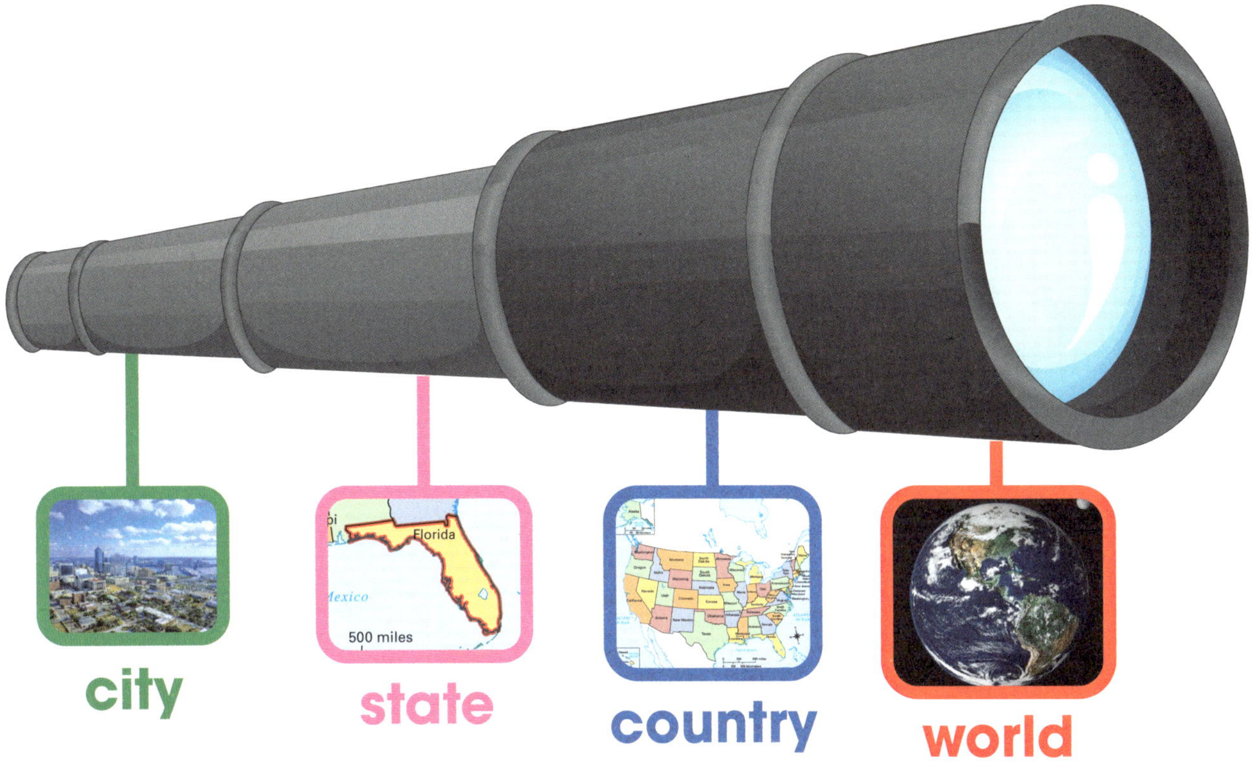


My ____________ is a place that I can see.

My ____________ is bigger with many cities.

My ____________ has 50 states.

My ____________ is every city, state, and country.

## Vocabulary Activity

Activity Online

Connect the word to the picture that shows it.

**city**

**state**

**country**

**world**

## Hands-On Activity

Make a telescope that shows your city, state, country, and the world. Use it to look at images and explain what they show. Then play a game that challenges you to categorize images as either a city, state, country, or the world.

### Directions: Finding My Place in the World

1. **With your partner, cut out your telescope.**
2. **Review the information on each slide.** Be sure to click on the pictures and audio to learn as much as you can.
3. **Read the matching section of text as you move through each slide.**
4. **Then draw on your telescope to show what you learned about where you are in the world.**
5. **Roll up your telescope.** You will use it to look at photos in the Where in the World Circle Game.

### Directions: Where in the World Circle Game

1. **Look at the four circles your teacher has drawn to represent a city, a state, a county, and the world.** The smallest circle in the middle represents a city. The next circles are for a state and then a country. The largest circle is the world.
2. **Study the image on the card your teacher holds up.** Is it a city, state, country, or the world?
3. **When your teacher says "go," move to the circle that matches the card.** Your teacher will place the card in the correct circle. Did you get it right?
4. **Play again!** Keep playing until all the cards have been played.

## 1. Living in a City

I live with my family in a **city**.

Here, there are tall buildings.

I see trees and bridges.

What is in your city?

In the summer, it is warm.

I have picnics in the park.

In the winter, it gets colder.

What do you do in the winter?

## 2. Living in a State

My city is in a **state**.

It has rivers and lakes.

Palm trees are a symbol of my state.

What are the symbols of your state?

There are many things to do.

I can go to a museum.

I can camp at a state park.

What can you do in your state?

## 3. Living in a Country

I live in the United States.

It is a **country**. Look at this map.

Find your state. Is it in the north,

south, east, or west?

## 4. Living in the World

I live in the **world**.

This is a picture of the world.

The blue parts show water.

What do the other colors show?

## Summary

I live in a city that is in a state.

My state is in a country in the world.

## Show What You Know

Circle the city.

Circle the state.

Circle the country.

Circle the world.

# Activity Cutouts

Activity Online

Cut out this telescope.

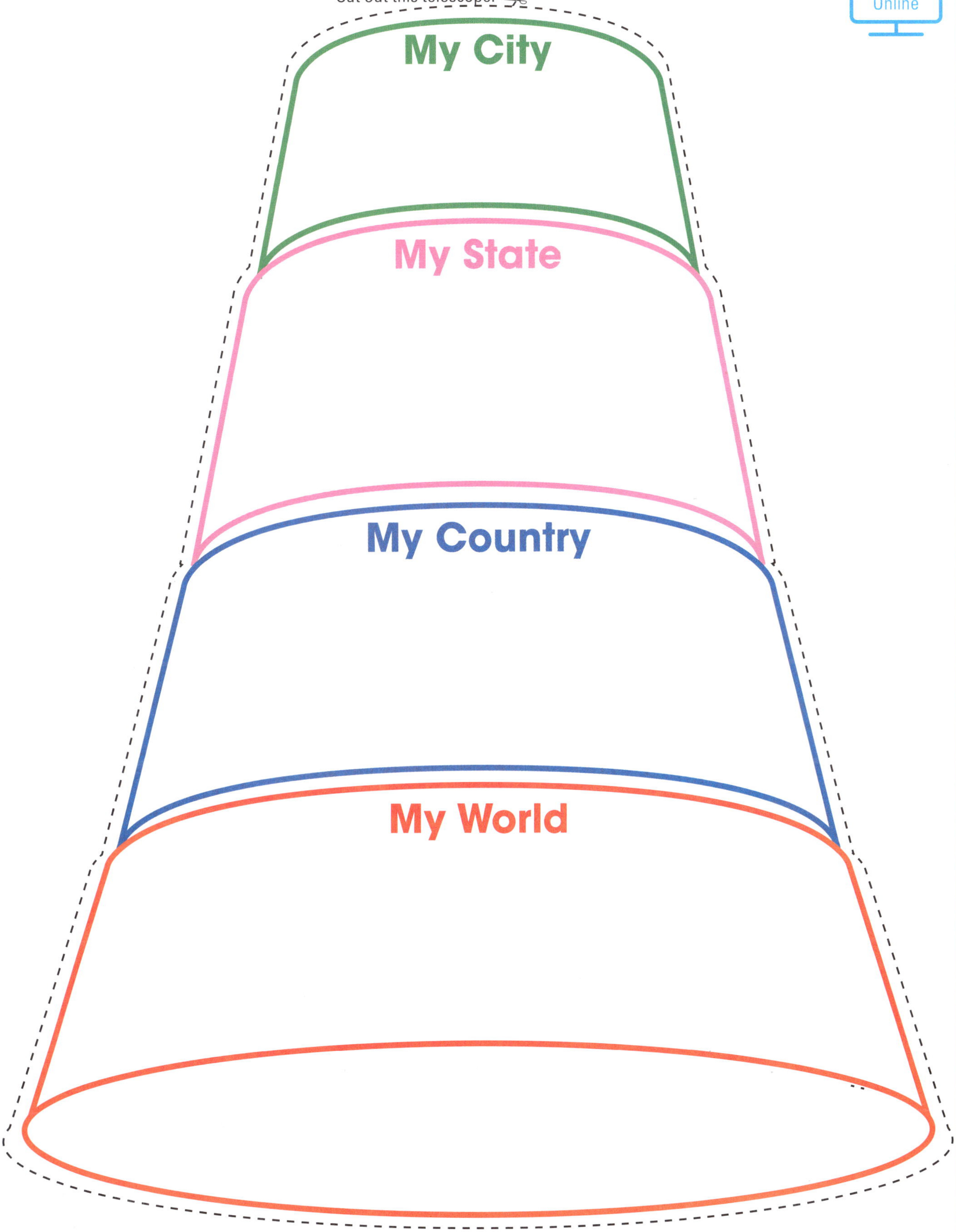

Tear out this page when you're ready to cut out your telescope.

# Lesson 11

# How Do People Live Around the World?

People live in

different places.

How do they live?

**Vocabulary**

**language**

**law**

Activity Online

Where are these students from? Draw a line from each student to their country.

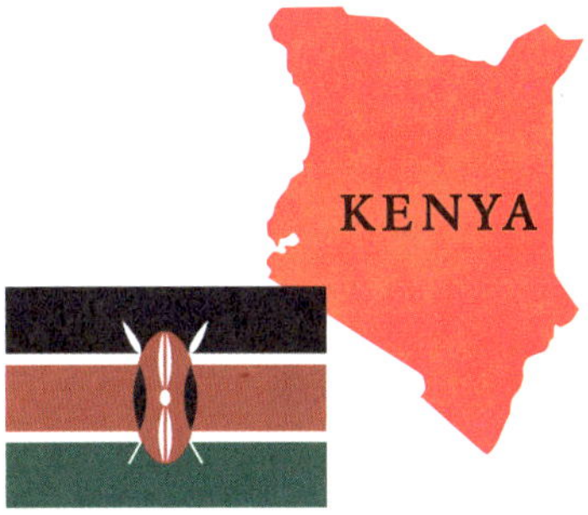

## Vocabulary Activity

Activity Online

Trace the word to finish each sentence.

My family can speak two languages!

We speak Spanish and English.

I follow the law. It helps me stay safe.

## Hands-On Activity

Activity Online

Prepare for a cultural fair by learning how four students eat, learn, play, and listen to music around the world.

### Directions: Discovering How People Live Around the World

1. **Learn more about our four new friends, their countries, and how they live.**
   - How do people around the world learn?
   - How do people around the world eat?
   - How do people around the world play?
   - How do people around the world listen to music?
2. **Go through each slide and read the matching section of text.**
3. **Complete your Activity Notes for the slide "Learn."**
4. **Create a piece of art to display at your cultural fair.** When you are finished, show it to your classmates.

## 1. People Talk to Each Other

All over the world, people talk.

They greet each other.

They say "hello" when they meet.

They say "goodbye" when they leave.

But all people do not speak

the same **language**.

They may say "nĭ haŏ" for "hello."

They may say "adios" for "goodbye."

## 2. Children Learn

Children in all places learn.

They learn to read and write.

They study math and science.

They may learn new languages.

But schools are not all the same.

Some schools meet on Saturday.

Classes can be big or small.

Students may dress the same.

## Hands-On Activity Notes

Trace the words for "hello" in each language.

Activity Online

### Practice writing "hello" in Turkish.

merhaba merhaba

### Practice writing "hello" in Chinese.

你好 你好 你好

### Practice writing "hello" in Swahili.

jambo jambo jambo

### Practice writing "hello" in Spanish.

hola hola hola

## 3. People Eat Together

Many families eat together.

But meals may be different.

Some people eat with a fork.

Others eat with chopsticks.

## 4. Children Play

All children love to play.

Games may be the same, or not.

Hopscotch in one country may look different in other places.

## 5. People Like Music

All people listen to music.

But the music may be different.

People can hear panpipes in Peru

or bagpipes in Scotland.

## 6. People Follow Laws

Countries have **laws,** or rules.

Laws are different in each place.

People drive on the right here.

In England, people drive on the left.

## Hands-On Activity Notes

Activity Online

Choose something you learned about how people live in Mexico, China, Kenya, or Turkey. Draw a picture for the cultural fair.

Circle the word that shows what your drawing is about.

learn    eat    play    music

## Summary

People talk, learn, eat, and play in different ways.

### Show What You Know

Pick a topic you learned about: eating, learning, playing, or listening to music. Choose two countries to compare, and draw a picture of your topic for each country.

| Country's Name | Country's Name |
| --- | --- |

Unit 4

# Economics

Go on a shopping trip to pick out things you need and want. Use your environmental superhero powers to find ways to protect Earth. Conduct an inquiry to figure out how to meet your needs while also helping our world.

# Unit Inquiry Project

## 1 Gathering Visual Evidence

| | |
|---|---|
| List five things you see in this photo. | |
| What are the students doing? What are they floating on? | |
| What items did they use to make their boat? Where might they have found these items? | |

 

## 2 Developing the Compelling Question

### Unit Storyline

This photo was taken in the Philippines in Asia. The students are in a competition. They were creative! They used old water bottles to build a boat. If there was a flood, the boat could help keep them safe. What other old items could be used to build a boat?

### Unit Compelling Question

*How can I meet my needs while taking care of our world?*

List three questions you have about the Unit Storyline and Compelling Question.

1.

2.

3.

## 3 Collecting Evidence

After you complete each lesson, return to this table and answer the questions. Record key information that will help you complete the Unit Inquiry Project.

| Lesson | Supporting Questions | What I Learned |
| --- | --- | --- |
| **12 What Do People Need and Want?** | Look at the photo again. Where do you see people meeting their needs?<br><br>How do you meet your needs and wants? | |
| **13 How Can I Help Take Care of the World?** | How are the people in the photo taking care of the world?<br><br>What are ways that you can reduce, reuse, and recycle? | |

## 4 Building Additional Content Knowledge

Gather and evaluate additional sources to answer the Unit Compelling Question: *How can I meet my needs while taking care of our world?*

You may conduct research or use these readings from *Social Studies Alive! Me and My World* Social Studies Stories:

- I Make Choices When I Shop
- Saving Money

| | |
|---|---|
| Source Title(s) | |
| Additional Evidence | |

## 5 Constructing an Argument

Write a sentence answering the Unit Compelling Question: *How can I meet my needs while taking care of our world?* This is called a claim.

Then give at least two pieces of evidence to support your claim. Your evidence can come from the activities you did in class, the readings you completed in your Student Journal or Social Studies Stories, or additional research that you conducted.

**Claim:**

**Evidence:**

## 6 Taking Informed Action

Decide how you want to share what you learned. You could make a poster, a presentation, or a video. You might share your presentation with your classmates or with adults in the community.

# Lesson 12

# What Do People Need and Want?

All people have needs.

They meet their needs in

different ways.

**Vocabulary**

**needs**

**shelter**

**wants**

## Preview Activity

Activity Online

You have 10 tokens to spend on fruit. Circle the fruits that you would like to buy. You must spend all 10 tokens.

## Vocabulary Activity

Activity Online

Trace the word to finish each sentence.

People all around the world have needs.

People need food, clothing, and shelter.

People in all places have different wants.

## Hands-On Activity

Go on a shopping trip and pick out new things you need and want. Then take your new things to the park to see what you can use.

### Directions: Going on a Shopping Trip

1. **Sit with your partner to prepare for a shopping trip.** You will help each other shop.
2. **Review all the things you can buy.** Your teacher will answer questions about the things you see in the store.
3. **Circle all the things you would buy.** You have 10 tokens to spend.
4. **Review what you bought.** Prepare to explain to the class what you purchased and why.

### Directions: Learning the Difference Between Needs and Wants

1. **With your partner, look at all the things you bought.** Are your items the same or different from your partner?
2. **Go to the playground and use your new things!**
3. **Read Sections 1–6.** Learn about needs and wants. What did you buy that you needed? What did you buy that you wanted?
4. **Talk to your partner about the things you bought that you could use at the park.** Did you have anything to play with, to eat, to keep you warm, and to protect you at night?
5. **Share what you discussed.**

## Hands-on Activity Notes

Activity Online

You have 10 tokens to spend on anything you see here. Circle the number of tokens each item costs. You must spend all 10 tokens.

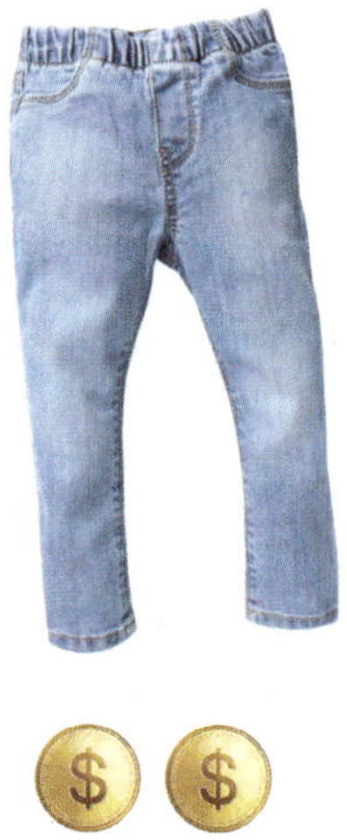

CANDY WORLD

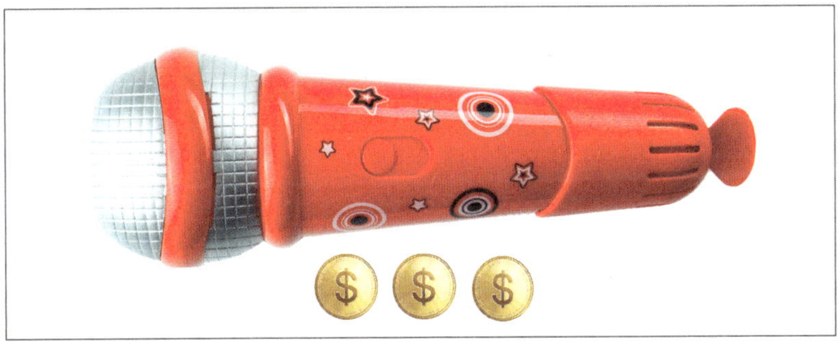

Stay for one night!

## 1. We Have Needs

All around the world,
people have **needs**.
A need is something
people must have to live.

## 2. We Need Food

People in all places need food.

They get food in different ways.

Some buy fruits and vegetables.

Some grow food on a farm.

## 3. We Need Clothing

People all around the world

need clothes to wear.

In cold places, they may wear coats.

In warm places, they may wear shorts.

## 4. We Need Shelter

All people need **shelter**.

Some people buy a house.

Or they rent a place to live.

Some build their own home.

## 5. We Have Wants

People in all places
have different **wants**.
A want is something people
like but do not need.

## 6. We Want Different Things

Some children want a book.

Others want new markers.

We cannot get all of our wants.

What do you want?

## Summary

We need food, clothing, and shelter.

We all want different things.

### Show What You Know

Write or draw a picture of one thing you need.

Write or draw a picture of one thing you want.

## Lesson 13

# How Can I Help Take Care of the World?

We all live on Earth.

We need to care for it.

How can I help?

**Vocabulary**

**garbage**

**recycle**

**reduce**

**reuse**

## Preview Activity

Activity Online

Circle the areas where we could help care for Earth.

## Vocabulary Activity

Activity Online

Trace the word to finish each sentence.

Gabi Garbage helps pick up garbage on Earth.

Bruce Reduce helps people reduce waste.

Lulu Reuse has ideas on how to reuse items.

Michael Recycle teaches us how to recycle.

## Hands-On Activity

Use your environmental superhero powers to find ways to protect Earth by reducing, reusing, and recycling the things you use every day.

### Directions: Rescuing Our World from Harm

1. **Read Sections 1–4.** Learn about ways we can help Earth.
2. **With your partner, you will receive a Green Family Superhero card.** You will get Gabi Garbage, Bruce Reduce, Lulu Reuse, or Michael Recycle. What does your superhero do?
3. **Look carefully at the slide and discuss how the superhero can help rescue our world from environmental harm.**
4. **When your superhero is on a slide, your teacher will tell you to go to the front of the classroom.** Join others who have your superhero!
5. **Share your ideas with the rest of the class.**

## 1. Less Garbage

All people throw away **garbage**.

There is so much waste!

It can harm the land.

I should try to make less garbage.

## 2. Reducing

I can **reduce** my trash.

I can throw away less.

I use the same lunch box.

I refill my water bottle.

## 3. Reusing

I can **reuse** my things.

An old sock is now a puppet.

My dad reuses an old tire.

The tire is now my swing.

## 4. Recycling

I can **recycle** plastic and glass.

I can recycle cans and paper.

They are made into new things.

A bottle can be made into a jar.

## Hands-On Activity Notes

Activity Online

Draw a line from each picture to the correct word.

**reduce**

**reuse**

**garbage**

**recycle**

## Summary

I can help take care of the world.

I can reduce, reuse, and recycle.

### Show What You Know

Write and draw a picture of one way you can reduce, reuse, or recycle. Tear this page out to make a poster.

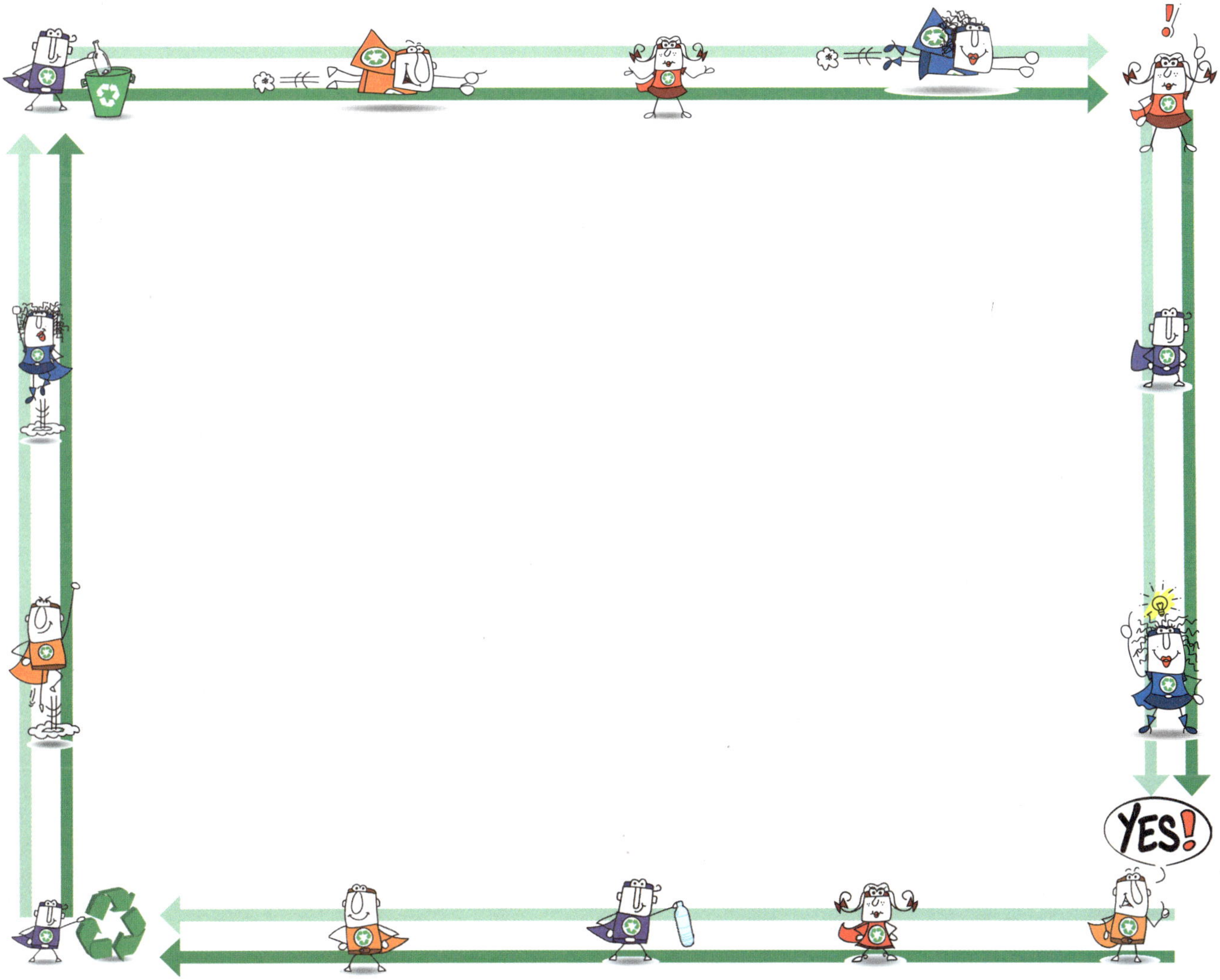

Tear out this page after you
have made your poster.

# United States Map

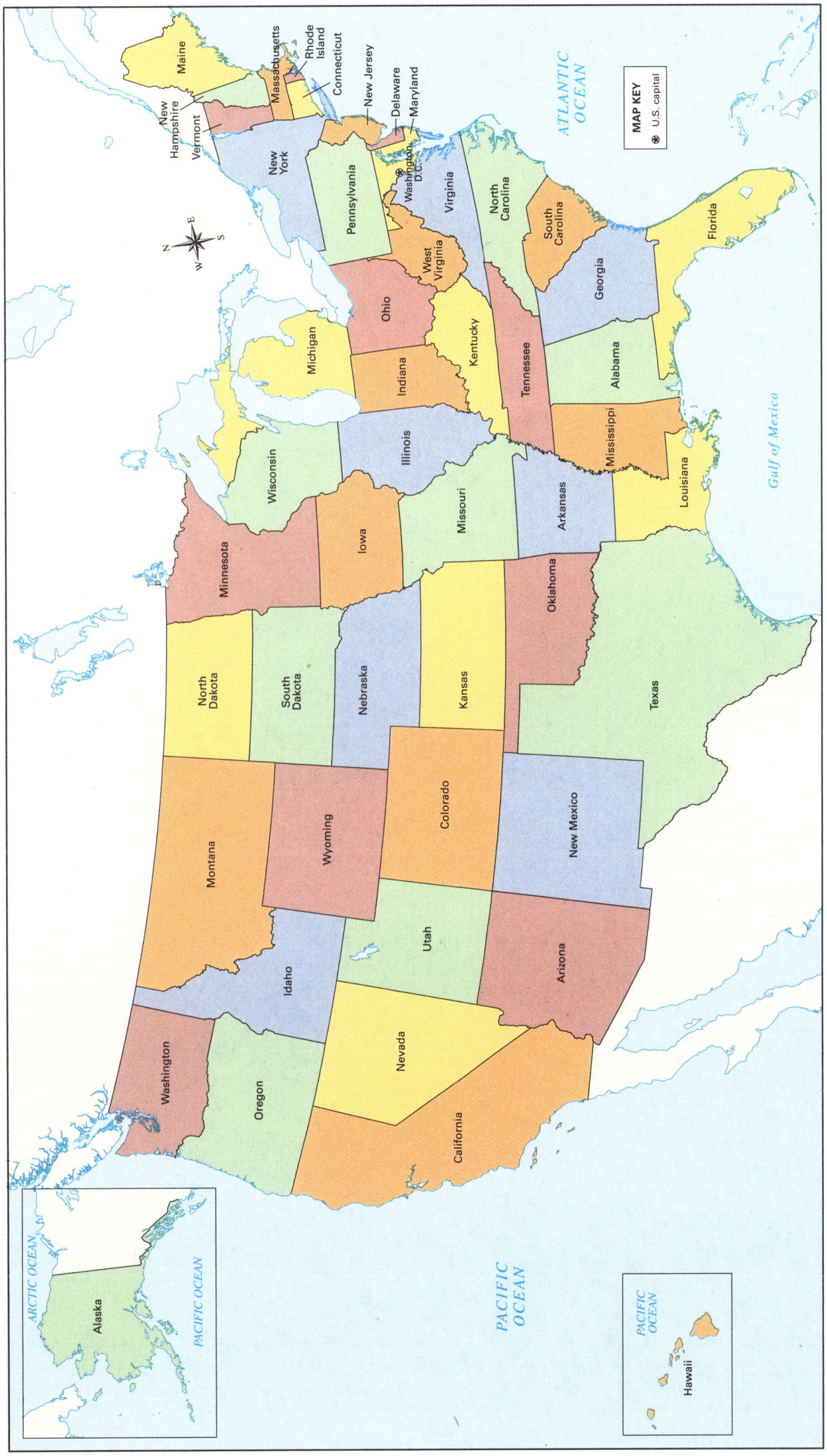

# World Map

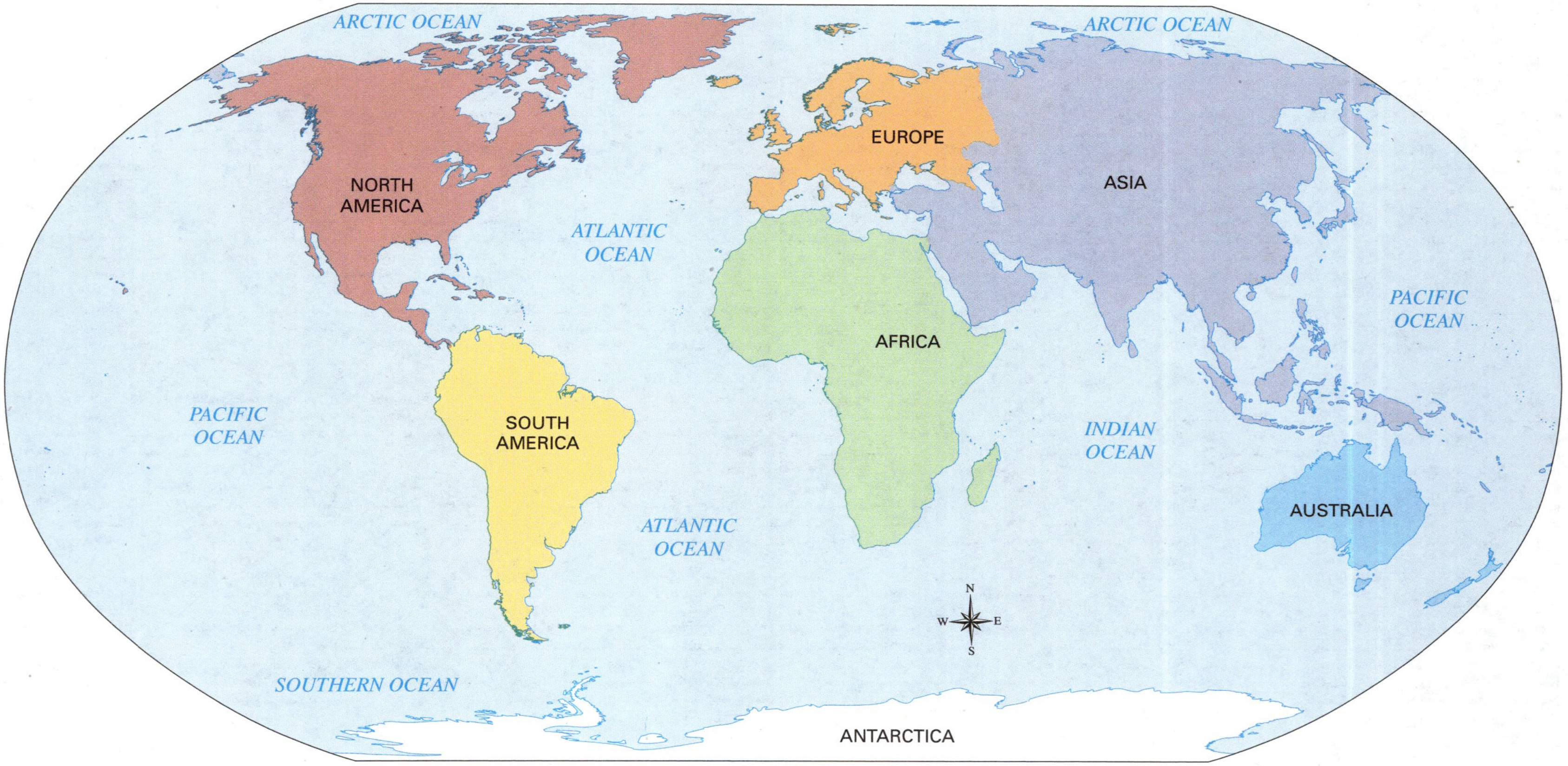
ARCTIC OCEAN
ARCTIC OCEAN
NORTH AMERICA
EUROPE
ASIA
ATLANTIC OCEAN
PACIFIC OCEAN
AFRICA
PACIFIC OCEAN
SOUTH AMERICA
INDIAN OCEAN
AUSTRALIA
ATLANTIC OCEAN
N
W
E
S
SOUTHERN OCEAN
ANTARCTICA

## calm down

## city

## country

## directions

## family

## federal holiday

## feelings

## garbage

## get along

## introduce

## language

## law

## map

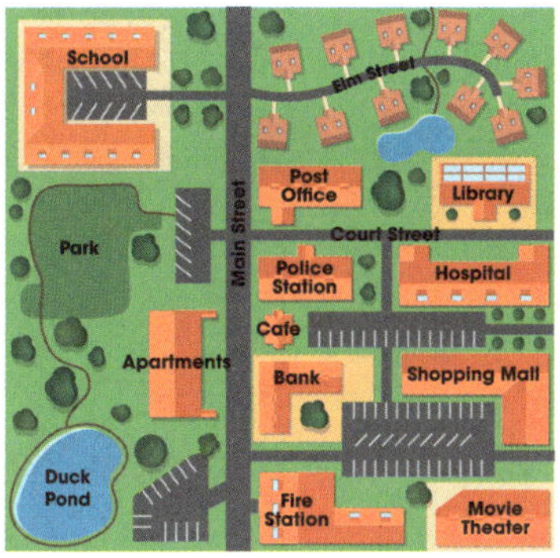


## needs

## neighbor

## neighborhood

## patriotic

## problem

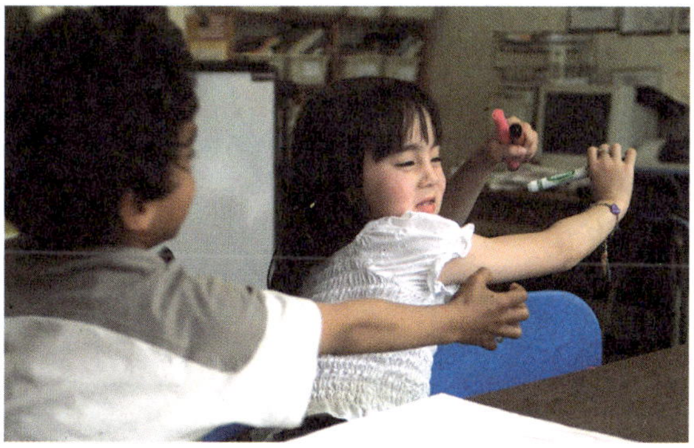

## recycle

## reduce

## reuse

## shelter

## solve

## special

## state

## tradition

## travel

## vote

## wants

## well

## world

# CREDITS

**Cover**
Getty Images

**Unit 1 Opener**
**1:** Library of Congress

**Lesson 1**
**7:** Thinkstock **9T:** MidoSemsem / Adobe Stock **9C:** Jaimie Duplass / Adobe Stock **9B:** Angelov / Adobe Stock **11:** Gelpi / Adobe Stock **11:** Pixabay **12:** iStockphoto **13:** Thinkstock **15:** Dreamstime **16:** Shutterstock

**Lesson 2**
**19:** Andy Dean / Adobe Stock Images **21:** Tartila / Adobe Stock Images **22T:** Thinkstock **22B:** Thinkstock **23:** Shutterstock **23:** wckiw / Adobe Stock Images **23:** ikostudio / Adobe Stock Images **24:** Thinkstock **25:** Thinkstock **26:** Monkey Business Images / Dreamstime.com **27BL:** Thinkstock **27R:** Thinkstock **28:** Thinkstock/SuperStock **29L:** Thinkstock **29R:** Copyright Redlink/Corbis/AP Images **30:** iStockphoto **31:** TCI **32:** Shutterstock

**Lesson 3**
**33T:** Shutterstock **33B:** Shutterstock **35TR:** Library of Congress **35BL:** Library of Congress **35BR:** Library of Congress **37:** junce11 / Adobe Stock Images **37:** altanaka / Adobe Stock Images **38:** iStockphoto **39B:** iStockphoto **40T:** Shutterstock **40C:** Shutterstock **40B:** Fotosearch.com **42:** Library of Congress **43:** David Mcshane | Dreamstime **44TL:** Fotosearch.com **44TR:** Shutterstock **44CL:** Shutterstock **44CR:** Shutterstock **44BL:** Shutterstock **44BR:** Shutterstock **45L:** gstockstudio / Adobe Stock **45R:** Library of Congress **46TL:** Shutterstock **46TR:** Shutterstock **46BL:** Dzmitry **46BR:** Dzmitry

**Unit 2 Opener**
**47:** JackF / Adobe Stock

**Lesson 4**
**53:** Thinkstock **55:** Shutterstock **56:** ONYXprj / Adobe Stock **56:** ONYXprj / Adobe Stock **57:** pressmaster / Adobe Stock **58:** Thinkstock **59:** Goldenkb/ Dreamstime **60:** Thinkstock **63:** Monkey Business **64:** ONYXprj / Adobe Stock

**Lesson 5**
**65:** Shutterstock **67:** Shutterstock **67:** Shutterstock **67:** Shutterstock **68TL:** Colorfuel Studio / Adobe Stock **68BL:** Colorfuel Studio / Adobe Stock **68CL:** Colorfuel Studio / Adobe Stock **68TR:** Colorfuel Studio / Adobe Stock **68CCR:** Colorfuel Studio / Adobe Stock **68BR:** Colorfuel Studio / Adobe Stock **69:** edward_indy / Adobe Stock **70:** Androniques / Dreamstime **71:** Getty Images **73:** TCI **74:** iStockphoto **75:** GraphicsRF / Adobe Stock **76:** ONYXprj / Adobe Stock

**Lesson 6**
**77:** Thinkstock **77:** Gelpi / Adobe Stock **79TR:** Fotosearch.com **79BR:** Fotosearch.com **79CL:** Fotosearch.com **79TL:** Fotosearch.com **79BL:** weedezign / Adobe Stock **79CR:** Foto2u / Adobe Stock **80T:** TCI **80TC:** TCI **80BC:** TCI **80B:** TCI **81:** Brocreative / Adobe Stock **82T:** TCI **82BL:** TCI **83T:** TCI **85T:** TCI **86T:** Fotosearch.com **87L:** Getty Images **87R:** Getty Images

**Lesson 7**
**91:** Cultura Creative (RF)/Alamy **93:** YummyBuum / Adobe Stock **93:** YummyBuum / Adobe Stock **94T:** jovannig / Adobe Stock **94B:** Idanupong / Adobe Stock **95:** mangpor2004 / Adobe Stock **96:** iStockphoto **97T:** bigmouse108 / Adobe Stock **97T:** sytnik / Adobe Stock **97T:** Andrey Nikitin / Adobe Stock **97T:** Alex Stemmer / Adobe Stock **97T:** Jon Anders Wiken / Adobe Stock **97T:** Татьяна Пинкасевич / Adobe Stock **97T:** dwi / Adobe Stock **97B:** Scanrail / Adobe Stock **97B:** donatas1205 / Adobe Stock **97B:** donatas1205 / Adobe Stock **97B:** sveta / Adobe Stock **97B:** Yio / Adobe Stock **97B:** AldanNa / Adobe Stock **97B:** ONYXprj / Adobe Stock **97B:** henrypark / Adobe Stock **97B:** henrypark / Adobe Stock **97B:** JSD / Adobe Stock **97B:** JSD / Adobe Stock **97B:** Tutsi_N / Adobe Stock **97B:** ttjanka / Adobe Stock **97B:** partyvector / Adobe Stock **97B:** toer / Adobe Stock **97B:** toer / Adobe Stock **98L:** iStockphoto **98R:** iStockphoto **99T:** Africa Studio / Adobe Stock **99T:** Rashevskyi Media / Adobe Stock **99T:** Asya / Adobe Stock **99T:** Coprid / Adobe Stock **99T:** Dmitri Stalnuhhin / Adobe Stock **99T:** Coprid / Adobe Stock **99T:** AVD / Adobe Stock **99T:** mbongo / Adobe Stock **99T:** graja / Adobe Stock **99T:** Nikolai Sorokin / Adobe Stock **99T:** Africa Studio / Adobe Stock **99T:** mbongo / Adobe Stock **99T:** Gennadiy Poznyakov / Adobe Stock **99B:** Peace / Adobe Stock **99B:** smile3377 / Adobe Stock **99B:** indigolotos / Adobe Stock **99B:** Yeti Studio / Adobe Stock **99B:** koosen / Adobe Stock **99B:** rimglow / Adobe Stock **99B:** picsfive / Adobe Stock **99B:** RTimages / Adobe Stock **99B:** chones / Adobe Stock **99B:** Coprid / Adobe Stock **100:** iStockphoto **101T:** Dvarg / Adobe Stock **101T:** pogonici / Adobe Stock **101T:** lilkin / Adobe Stock **101T:** Svetlana Nikolaeva / Adobe Stock **101T:** BetterStock / Adobe Stock **101T:** david_franklin / Adobe Stock **101T:** Suraphol / Adobe Stock **101T:** Artem Shadrin / Adobe Stock **101T:** avtk / Adobe Stock **101T:** avtk / Adobe Stock **101T:** avtk / Adobe Stock **101T:** Jenny / Adobe Stock **101T:** DNY3D / Adobe Stock **101T:** Africa Studio / Adobe Stock **101T:** michaklootwijk / Adobe Stock **101B:** taonga / Adobe Stock **101B:** moodboard / Adobe Stock **101B:** Monkey Business / Adobe Stock **101B:** Monkey Business / Adobe Stock **101B:** pololia / Adobe Stock **101B:** oksix / Adobe Stock **101B:** davit85 / Adobe Stock **101B:** New Africa / Adobe Stock **101B:** Africa Studio / Adobe Stock **101B:** Robert Kneschke / Adobe Stock **101B:** Rawpixel.com / Adobe Stock **101B:** Monkey Business / Adobe Stock **101B:** New Africa / Adobe Stock **102:** iStockphoto **103T:** imagesbykenny / Adobe Stock **103B:** chiaro85 / Adobe Stock **104:** klyaksun / Adobe Stock

## Lesson 8

**105:** Robert Kneschke / Adobe Stock **107BCR:** Fotosearch.com **107TCL:** Fotosearch.com **107BR:** Fotosearch.com **107TCR:** Fotosearch.com **107BCL:** Fotosearch.com **107TR:** Fotosearch.com **107BL:** Fotosearch.com **107TL:** Fotosearch.com **108B:** Glenda Powers / Adobe Stock **108T:** Andy Dean / Adobe Stock **109:** escapejaja / Adobe Stock **110:** Thinkstock **111:** Shutterstock **112L:** Shutterstock **113:** United States Postal Service **114:** Teresa Kenney / Dreamstime **115L:** Wikimedia **115R:** Wikimedia **116:** Thinkstock **117C:** Fotosearch.com **117B:** Fotosearch.com **117T:** Fotosearch.com **119TR:** Fotosearch.com **119BL:** Fotosearch.com **121BR:** Fotosearch.com **121CL:** Fotosearch.com **121TR:** Fotosearch.com **121TL:** Fotosearch.com **121BL:** Fotosearch.com

## Unit 3 Opener

**123:** burak / Adobe Stock

## Lesson 9

**129:** iStockphoto **131T:** drosostalitsa / Adobe Stock Images **131BR:** Veniamin Kraskov / Adobe Stock Images **131BLC:** Ammak / Adobe Stock Images **131BRC:** jan nakhonkae / Adobe Stock Images **131BL:** ThomasLENNE / Adobe Stock Images **132:** Satjawat / Adobe Stock Images **133:** pressmaster / Adobe Stock Images **134:** drosostalitsa / Adobe Stock Images **135L:** Thinkstock **135R:** Thinkstock **136T:** iStockphoto **136B:** Ellen Isaacs/Alamy **137TL:** Thinkstock **137R:** Thinkstock **137BL:** MBI/Alamy **138TL:** Africa Studio / Adobe Stock **138TR:** Monkey Business / Adobe Stock **138BL:** Rawpixel.com / Adobe Stock **138BR:** Mike Eikenberry / Adobe Stock **139:** AlexZel / Adobe Stock Images **140:** Seamartini/Dreamstime **141:** TCI **142L:** Golden Pixels LLC/Alamy **142R:** Barry Diomede/Alamy **143:** John Steel/Alamy

## Lesson 10

**145:** iStockphoto **147T:** GraphicsRF / Adobe Stock **149:** Pixel-shot / Alamy Stock Photo **149:** Pixabay **150:** Adobe Stock Images **151R:** Adobe Stock Images **151L:** Viktor Pravdica/Dreamstime **152TL:** Adobe Stock Images **152TR:** Adobe Stock Images **152BL:** iStockphoto **152BR:** Adobe Stock Images **153:** Thinkstock **154:** TCI **155:** iStockphoto **156TCR:** SeanPavonePhoto / Adobe Stock **156TCL:** Adobe Stock Images **156TCC:** pingebat / Adobe Stock **156TR:** Destina / Adobe Stock **156BCC:** pavalena / Adobe Stock **156TL:** pyty / Adobe Stock **156BC:** Pixabay **156TC:** Pixabay **156BR:** md3d / Adobe Stock **156BCR:** Pixabay **156BCL:** pingebat / Adobe Stock

## Lesson 11

**159:** Yan Liao/Alamy **161:** Gelpi / Adobe Stock **161:** Tarik GOK / Adobe Stock **161:** kornnphoto / Adobe Stock **161:** Archer7 / Adobe Stock **161:** paulmz / Adobe Stock **161:** pavlofox / Adobe Stock **161:** asem arab / Adobe Stock **161:** VectorPart / Adobe Stock **162T:** Rob / Adobe Stock **162BR:** denys_kuvaiev / Adobe Stock **162BL:** chekman / Adobe Stock **163:** Hello Cinthia / Adobe Stock **163:** Alex Green / Adobe Stock **164L:** Design Pics Inc / Alamy Stock Photo **164R:** Inmagine/Alamy **165:** Thinkstock **166:** iStockphoto **167:** Thinkstock **168T:** asem arab / Adobe Stock **168TC:** kornnphoto / Adobe Stock **168BC:** paulmz / Adobe Stock **168B:** Krakenimages.com / Adobe Stock **169:** iStockphoto **170L:** Greatstock Photographic Library/Alamy **170R:** PhotoAlto/Alamy **171L:** iStockphoto **171R:** Findlay/Alamy **172:** Thinkstock **173:** romantiche / Adobe Stock **174:** Lorelyn Medina / Adobe Stock

## Unit 4 Opener

**175:** REUTERS / Alamy Stock Photo

## Lesson 12

**181:** Dmitry Kalinovsky/Dreamstime **183:** Visual Generation / Adobe Stock **183BC:** gertrudda / Adobe Stock **183BL:** valery121283 / Adobe Stock **183TR:** Tim UR / Adobe Stock **183BR:** xamtiw / Adobe Stock **183TC:** Dionisvera / Adobe Stock **183TL:** atoss / Adobe Stock **184T:** Tartila / Adobe Stock **184C:** Tartila / Adobe Stock **184C:** Tartila / Adobe Stock **184C:** vectorikart / Adobe Stock **184C:** klyaksun / Adobe Stock **184B:** Shanvood / Adobe Stock **185:** Gelpi / Adobe Stock **186BL:** Gennady Poddubny / Adobe Stock **186CC:** abramsdesign / Adobe Stock **186BR:** wabeno / Adobe Stock **186CR:** nys / Adobe Stock **186TL:** Fotosearch.com **186CL:** Nikolai Sorokin / Adobe Stock **186BC:** Audrius Merfeldas / Adobe Stock **186TR:** lithiumphoto / Adobe Stock **187TL:** ValentinValkov / Adobe Stock **187BL:** sveta / Adobe Stock **187TCR:** lana_u / Adobe Stock **187BCR:** gertrudda / Adobe Stock **187TR:** canbedone / Adobe Stock **187BCL:** hadeev / Adobe Stock **187TC:** ImagesMy / Adobe Stock **187TCC:** Kuzmick / Adobe Stock **187BR:** Africa Studio / Adobe Stock **187TCL:** Olga / Adobe Stock **188RB:** Kmiragaya/Dreamstime **188RT:** Shutterstock **188L:** Shutterstock **189L:** Thinkstock **189R:** Thinkstock **190:** Ton Koene/VWPics/Alamy **191:** Thinkstock **192:** Cultura Creative RF / Alamy Stock Photo **193:** Deyangeorgiev/Dreamstime

## Lesson 13

**195:** iStockphoto **197T:** blueringmedia / Adobe Stock **197B:** YummyBuum / Adobe Stock **198T:** christophe BOISSON / Adobe Stock **198B:** christophe BOISSON / Adobe Stock **198TC:** christophe BOISSON / Adobe Stock **198BC:** christophe BOISSON / Adobe Stock **199:** evening_tao / Adobe Stock **200:** iStockphoto **201L:** Getty Images **201R:** Thinkstock **202:** iStockphoto **203:** Getty Images **204TL:** Africa Studio / Adobe Stock **204TL:** photka / Adobe Stock **204BCL:** Aleksey Butov / Adobe Stock **204BCL:** MRkringsak / Adobe Stock **204BL:** RTimages / Adobe Stock **204TCL:** cgdeaw / Adobe Stock